# DRIED DAISIES SPROUTING FROM MY DESK

A poetry collection
by Sophia-Maria Nicolopoulos

*In memory of*
*my GRANDMA SOPHIA*
February 1948–July 2022

*Losing you so quickly was earth-shattering. The death of a loved one is terrifying, and I never expected we wouldn't hug each other again. You never got the chance to hear that I'd launch my own chapbook or that I'm writing a lot these days. Please, know that I've already written stories and poems inspired by you. I started long before you passed away.*

*I will pray for you every single day.*

*I love you, too.*

Foreword

Poetry is an intuitive choice whenever I'm drowning in bouts of anxiety, fear, and self-doubt. It's been a lighthouse of all the weight I carry, and I want to exorcise, all those intimate details I'm afraid to share with the rest of the world. Sometimes, I still feel that my words have no room in contemporary poetry, but then I remember the tremendous fun I had writing down those first poems with the help of prompts and the genuine connections I've made with Instagram poets throughout 2021.

One of those poets is Faye Alexandra Rose, whose work I admire tremendously and whose editing of this chapbook improved my own skills as a new poet. I'm forever grateful for her constructive feedback and unparalleled support for my work, for she reminds me that friendships can be formed regardless of who you are, where you come from, and how you look.

Finally, this chapbook wouldn't have been a reality without the fantastic poetry prompts by Small Leaf Press. They were the ones that got me back to writing poetry after a three-year hiatus. I used to work two jobs during that time, and the never-ending quarantine had viciously attacked my mental health. Finding time to write down poetry with the help of prompts was what clicked for me then and calls to me now. While all poems found in this collection have been edited many times (some are also written as spin-offs of the original ones), I could have never finished a chapbook without Small Leaf's inspirational words.

This is a coming-of-age chapbook, and it should be read as your well-hidden diary, a collage of unexplained emotions and unnamed fears. It's also rooted in my unique experience growing up as a too sheltered, shy Greek kid. I hope it'll take you by the hand and safely walk you through the unscalable peaks of growing up.

Table of Contents

Father, forgive me—

*Originally published by Small Leaf Press in
Jaden Magazine (2021)

lying
under the
pine tree and
counting the soft shadows
recalling his warm eyes, furrowed
and billowy like his favorite sea
a shadow for each time he called me
"daughter,"
a needle for each time he proudly held my
childlike hand.
Father, forgive me; I'm tall but lonely,
words are utterly failing me,
I've used them all but left out four,
since the transparent waves are receding.
Let me wrap you with these hidden lines,
look at you; forever shrouded, deep within
the soggy soil,
IshouldhavecomeIshouldhavecomeIshouldha
vecomeIshouldhavecomeIshouldhavecome

Song: To my mother—

*I'm right here, mother, if you'd like to speak*
*to me,*
*really speak, I'm next to you—*

My mother dips her elegant fingers in
piquant Wine
consecrating my blood and body to a
towering vine,
her hands washing and treating with care
my nine-year-old Sunday skirt.

*I wish you could hear me; my voice cracks,*
*I have no more notes to play and not enough*
*words to find.*

She sports deep bruises and long cuts
from running around catching the rats
by flaying the plaster through the walls of
my dark-lit room,
creatures that always strike when she's away
in late afternoon.

*I wish you would visit me in my sleep,*
*tucking hair behind my ear, fixing my frown.*

My mother is the Lighthouse of my life
despite the thorns entangled around her
small knife,
and the choice of words that can deeply hurt,
she looks after my withered petals, blowing

away the painful dirt.

*I have so much more to tell you, so much*
*more to confess,*
*but you wouldn't want to see your daughter*
*a mess.*

She loves diving into the raging sea,
trampling over poisonous weeds
that threaten to infringe my dreams.

*That's why I'm keeping the song going,*
*giving you one last chance to see what you*
*expect*
*of me, the daughter you'd love to have—*

Mother fetches me a glass of water
whenever I ask,
placing a smiling mask
and chanting protection prayers taken by
Sunday Mass.

*Mom, are you there? Can you hear me?*
*Please say something!*

In essence, all I'm trying to say
is that my mother keeps me safe
with her own unorthodox ways,
she never fails to amaze me when she
willingly stays
by my side, even if I'm having one of those
"days."

*I love you even if you'd never say it back,*
*please don't go,*
*please don't—*

Oh, mother! I always thought
you weren't made
for this mortal-bound world!

*You said you'd never leave me alone! Come*
*back! Do you hear me? Wake up!*

I was supposed to wait for you—

with the thread around my fingers,
but, times have changed,
and so have my too timid, too quiet eyes.

The monster has run away, and I'm now
free.

Free to walk across the land;
free to fly against the lustful sea,
fearing no man will wrap me around his
finger, and no needle will penetrate me.

I'm terrified of—

unanswered questions
of childish fears
of a sense of staying alone
of masked truths passing as
pleasant lies.


I stand on the cliff bounded by
a boundless sense of dread by
immature shadows by
abandoned apparitions—

the ones that make you stay awake at night.


For long, I've stepped on dry leaves and
hidden thorns.
At least, up here, on the edge of my fear,
I'm thinking of how successful I am
to make it for another year.

Getting closer to the thirty—

now aged seven of twenty
being asked to sew dresses
for a boy or a girl
and then, to bake pies
for a husband.
I wonder;
When will the stars come down
to invite me to their celestial dance
and wrap me with stardust
and meteor ash?

I wonder;
When will my hands finally
let me go?
When will my hair grow
out of its mold?

Will I ever get out of this eternal loop?
Will I ever have my younger eyes back
or
Will I just perish
as a loving sister, a devout wife,
a sweet mother,
even a caring grandmother,
all in the name of going over thirty?

It is a monster—

of black tar eyes
there's no nose, only a mouth
hanging loose with rotten gums,
a horrid smell, a nasty look,
small pointy teeth
that when they come for me,
could take down my planet, too.

It's creeping up on me now,
desperate to take control,
the ooze I'm feeding for so long,
squeezing my limbs one by one,
ready to devour and steal their form.

This creature, this!
I must battle by myself,
I breathe in and out,
but only when its talons permit me.
Now, its breath licks my ears
derisively
distorting my sense of reality
of all's well,

whatifwhatifwhatifwhatifwhatif

S

T

O

P

I take my only weapon:
a breath,
a poem,
a story,
I weave them inside my exhausted mind
carefully laying out all the details,
silently praying, oh yes, praying for the
Light,

*Will no one hear the way I gasp
for air late at night?*


I toss and turn while he's sleeping.
It's not fair!
The creature pounces on me, but I MUST
carry ON!



I MUST!
I WILL!

Waking up to find out that I'm—

missing things
because I can't seem
to stop the racing thoughts
in my mind, which drown my insides.

Oh, how different would it be
if for one nanosecond, I closed my eyes
and asked the pit to take another one, not
me,
and it obeyed!

4 am/ 4 pm—

4 am

trapped under
the footsteps
of my dreams,
I'm thinking
of the key
but no key
sits on my palm.
There's a face
that makes me sweaty.
I run
but I'm deep
in the lair,
and he's above water
lazily breathing,
he can't hear the
voices, he can't see the
disjointed skeletal face
following me.

4 pm

the cutlery is shining
no need to use more
bleach.
I've washed away
the anxious tremors,
the irrational fears
of last night's sleep
but he still can't see my anguish,
he can't taste my pain.

I've always lived under the sea
breathing water and eating weeds.
I've always been attracted
to the abyss,
overthinking, scrutinizing, ruminating,
building castles on the octopus's back.

I dream of carelessness—

shattered wings in the mud
and fallen leaves next to fountains.

I dream of long walks under comets
and shooting stars;
there's a reason why I love tasting
wishful thinking.

I dream of all those kisses
I'll never give
and beds
I'll never share.
I dream of restless nights,
half-finished journals
and truancies,
so that I can run with my feet bare
and dive into the sea of unfulfilled wishes.

I dream of clouds that are far away
and suitcases that will never be packed.
I dream of sunsets in foreign lands
and smiles of unknown people, accents of
other blood
and hands that speak of thousand cuts.

I'll always dream of unfinished business,
feelings and experiences that I'll never
savor.

But that's the way of life,
choosing a road and cutting on all others,

following a route until its end
because you're too scared to even pull your
window on
and hit the gas.

Deadly nights like these—

where I curl my toes under the blanket
to numb the cold
and when the space next to me
even if occupied
feels cold –vacant—unattended,
my mind drifts to the what-ifs,
the enchanting fantasies I build and rebuild
for myself
where I'm not fulfilling
norms and rules
and I leave my tea getting cold,
dreams where I let my hair down,
and enjoy the damp streets,
naked and in need
of a broken heart.

Valentine's Day—

dust settles
on the yellow paper
(February 14th)
is circled
in ruby red
but there's no one left
to shake
the dry ballpoint pen.

Serotonin—

S ilently
E longating
R adiant
O live branches
T o
O rbit
N earby and around your
I ncredibly intricate
N ebula of scars.

September—

by the bus stop
around 9 pm,
your lips were cold
(perhaps stiffer then
and less soft as now)
mine were steeped in
self-doubt
and concern
but fused with excessive yearn.

Cuddling at night—

our cold toes interlocked,
my forehead trapped under your nose,
neither credit cards nor roses
certainly not jewelry
can account for the nature
of our love.

It tastes like mountainous water
and feels like oak moss
after spring rain
on your fingertips.

Today I will simply—

pretend
to be
a skylark
above a
foreign sea
making love
to the
uncanny desires
the waves
carry within.

Humble Moisture—

*The original version was first published in
the Autumn 2021 Anthology by Sunday
Mornings at the River*

glasses clinking
cocktail dresses swirling
gowns rustling

but once the music stops,
only the sound of the wind
kissing the clematis vines,
only the morning rain,
hugging the jasmine stems
urge my feet to walk by your side.

That's the way I choose to love you,
like the humble moisture does
with the tall grass.

There's an ethereal beauty—

in the trajectory
of rivulets on the
windshield window
while we're listening
to 80s hits
and crossing borders.

The Language of Love—

Tears
running
on
my cheeks

sweat
sitting
on
my lips

pain
piercing
my chest

warmth
surrounding
my
breasts

Summer melts on my skin—

the deteriorating process officially begins,
my pulse threatening me,
always spiking, and
teasing
laughing
pointing at me.

Summer melts on my skin
as I lay sunbathing,
the sound of the waves does little to comfort
me; the world so far has been a frightening
place.

Yet your fingers caress my own
and your lips touch my sweaty brow,
you smell of safety,
rosemary and daisies,
your tired arms
much longer and bigger
than mine.

You're holding me tightly,
gently squeezing me
while whispering,

*All's well in your state of uncertainty.*

Then, you say,

"Take deep breaths."
"Persevere."

The sand stills under my trembling hands
and I know,
in that insignificant, tiny fraction of a
moment,
I know I'll be held,
loved and
cherished.

You give me the power to push through;
your kiss so kind, it causes me to bloom.

*All's well in your state of uncertainty.*
*You're more than just a web of alarming*
*thoughts*
*and sleepless nights.*
*You're well. And will be.*

The shadows playfully bite my cheek—

but I turn the other way,
*Please, I'll give you anything!*

They are punctual,
constantly stopping by after midnight,
when his hands cannot warm me enough,
when his breathing slows.

Yet, my legs grow abnormally long,
*Just make it stop!*
They carry me on
through tides of lingering,
storms of remembering,
hails of self-punishing,

*No, I won't let go!*
The shadows devour me,
and shred me alive,
digging their nails into my pale skin,
dancing on my raw flesh,
feasting on my sex.

One sheep,
Two,
three—


—he wakes up and tucks me in.

"Hold on to my pinkie like this—

and promise you'll stay by my side,
and I'll slay gorgons and sirens for you,
and even pour my own blood out
just to make sure you survive."

Wistfully looking—

for the gradual renewal of my leaves
and the blossoming of my frosty petals,
I welcome spring,
with moist running on my stem,
faithfully waiting
to replant my roots
in fresh soil.

Walking in spring—

soft air
tracing
kisses on my hair,
sudden rain
pouring,
flooding my hooded eyelids graciously,
the first shred of hope
in people's smiles,
chucking
giggling
laughing
blushed cheeks counting
the heart rate of refreshing love,
humble ants waking up from their icy
slumber,
native tulips finding their place under
the friendly sun,
the green landscape
bristles with ladybugs
walking on coreopsis,
thousands of chances for caterpillars
to spread their patterns,
and shake off their dust
day after day.

I belong to this humble world,
as a tiny seed among millions of others,
or a sprout needing lovely water,
and plenty of sun to grow old.

Take care of your carpet—

for it remembers,
its memory foam
permanently molding and reshaping,
once you wake up,
it traps all the footsteps
and the palms
that left an imprint in your heart,
it holds onto your wrappers,
bottle tops and clipped nails,
it's your diary of pie crust
and unfulfilled birthday wishes,
it holds onto the music
that escorted you throughout the good
and the bad.

Take care of your carpet
for it remembers,
its memory foam is determined
to survive
being shaped by all the tears,
the piercing screams,
and useless pills
you've just stepped on.

Letter to my writer self—

*First published in the Autumn 2021
Anthology by Sunday Mornings at the River.*

Words will fail you,
emotions, like the billowy sea,
will sweep you away,
but you'll stay on course
navigating the crimson walls,
the deepest seabed,
you'll walk on its delicate thorns
crushing rusty nails and lost journals.
You'll dive into bottomless pits,
naked, with only your heart as your guide,
triumphantly salvaging cursed treasures,
and maps to forbidden houses.

Words will fail you,
and so will people,
time and again,
but you're born to be more than a captain,
your eyes, thirsty,
and filled with unwritten stories.

Yes, you're the humble sailor,
who had the courage and the tenacity
to grab those lurid nightmares,
sipping their nectar
and spilling her ink for them.

You're a cartographer, and you'll create
wor(l)ds
whenever others abandon you,
leaving you beaten and bruised at the far-
right corner
of your old ship.

About the Author

Sophia-Maria Nicolopoulos is a Content and Publishing Editor from Greece. She holds a BA with distinction in English Language & Literature from the National University of Athens and an MA in English & American Studies from the Aristotle University of Thessaloniki.

She chooses to see her work as the kind a Greek Ophelia would write had she navigated a world of boundless horror. She writes to make sense of the obscure places where reality meets the surreal.

She hates the taste of fresh tomatoes, but she loves cheese. In her free time, she removes cat hair from her clothes.

This is her first poetry chapbook. She is known as @lostlenore_ on Instagram and as @sophiam_weaves on Twitter. These are the two places she talks about reading, writing, editing, and how supreme beings cats are.

For further information on her work and services, find her at:

https://sophiamarianicolopoulos.wordpress.com

Cover Design & Illustrations by Kalli Karapanou @kalli_k_ on Instagram.

Printed in Great Britain
by Amazon